THE COMPLETE GUIDE TO PRIZE WINNING

by
Linda Evanston

SANTA MONICA PRESS
P.O. Box 1076
Santa Monica, CA 90406-1076
Printed in the United States
All Rights Reserved

TABLE OF CONTENTS

INTRODUCTION

Millions of Dollars to be Won

Each year, millions of dollars are won in sweepstakes and contests by people just like you. Most people are very skeptical about such games, feeling that you simply can't get something for nothing. These people feel it is not worth their time or effort to enter, and they often resort to the time-worn excuse, "No one really wins anyway." But this could not be further from the truth. You can rest assured that most sweepstakes and contests are completely legitimate, that there are very few incidents of fraud or cheating, and that the winners are almost never friends of the judges.

But why does it always seem like some-body else wins? Quite simply, because most people just don't have the discipline to become a winner. How often have you been reluctant to enter a sweepstake or contest just because you didn't think you would win? But how can you possibly win if you don't even enter? Participating in sweep-stakes and contests should be looked at like a hobby; you're not going to get good at it unless you devote plenty of time to it. Some people are even able to turn their hobby into a profession, winning so many sweepstakes and contests that they can quit their regular jobs and devote all of their time to entering such promotions. They are able to win with surprising consistency, earning houses, cars, money, and other prizes. The IRS even recognizes prize winnings as a legitimate source of income.

But before continuing with the idea of winning prizes, the main point of this book, let's quickly return to the attitude you should take as a sweepstake and contest entrant. Once again, you should think of it as a hobby. Entering sweepstakes and contests, like any other hobby, is something to be enjoyed in your free time. You should relish the tension of waiting until the winners are announced; you should fantasize about the day you will become a winner, quit your job, and move to a tropical island; you should dream of sitting down behind the wheel of that Ferrari you always wanted; and you should forget all of the troubles from the office as you tirelessly devote yourself to filling out entry forms at night. In short, you should enjoy the process of entering sweepstakes and contests, and not just its rewards. That way, you can never be a loser. Your life will be enriched by spending your free time doing something you find truly entertaining. Being a sweepstake and contest entrant is much like watching sporting events on TV: while we often hope for a certain outcome, most of the joy actually comes from simply watching the event.

Keeping that in mind, let us return to the rewards. The rewards are there to be won, and they are sometimes more exciting, exotic, and expensive than you would ever dare imagine. Italian sports cars, custom built houses, millions of dollars in cash, and many other prizes are regularly given away in sweepstakes and contests. While it is impossible to guarantee that you can become a winner, let alone one of the frequent winners described above, you can significantly increase your chances by following the suggestions outlined in this book.

The first two suggestions both have to do with attitude. By now you already know what the first one is: don't be afraid to enter. Enter as often as possible. Don't allow yourself to be overcome by fears of losing; even the regular winners lose more frequently than they win, and sometimes the most you have to lose is the price of postage. Remind yourself that people really do win.

The second suggestion is to do your home-work. Many people never achieve the level of excellence they desire in their hobbies because they aren't willing to put the neces-sary time into it. All hobbies take time, and entering sweepstakes and contests is no exception. By doing your homework, I mean that you should take the time to learn the rules of different sweepstakes and contests. Are you allowed to enter more than once? Is any purchase necessary? Should you type or print the entry form? In fact, it is estimated that at least twenty-five percent to perhaps as many as ninety per-cent of all sweepstake and contest entries are thrown out because they don't follow the rules. Think of how greatly your chances are increased if you just spend the extra time reading all of the rules!

Sweepstakes versus Contests

You're probably aware of the words sweepstakes and contests, but you don't really understand how they differ from each other. This section will discuss their differences, as well as their relative advantages and disadvantages; in a way, you can consider this section your first homework assignment.

It is easier to define sweepstakes and contests by starting with their more familiar grandfather -- the lottery. A lottery is any game which consists of three elements. These three elements are chance (luck), the entry fee (sometimes referred to as the consideration), and the prize. The first element, that of luck, is introduced by the very fact that you are competing against thousands of other people by predicting several numbers that will be chosen at random. The entry fee is generally the price of the ticket itself. Most lottery tickets cost one dollar. And the prizes are usually money.

What differentiates a sweepstake or contest from a lottery is that one of the three elements has been removed. In a sweepstake, that element is the entry fee. In other words, the game is still a game of chance, and there are still prizes to be won (although not necessarily cash prizes), but you don't have to pay to enter.

Contests, on the other hand, retain the element of the entry fee, but remove luck. The entry fee is usually in the form of purchasing one or more of a company's products. For example, a contest often requires you to send in a proof of purchase or a label; obviously, you cannot obtain these items without buying the product. It does not matter whether you personally bought it, or if one of your friends purchased it.

The luck is removed by adding a requirement of skill. Whereas sweepstakes are determined through random drawings, contests require the participants to perform in some way. A contest may ask you to write a song, or make a rhyme, or even explain why you use a product. A panel of judges then determines which contestant they feel has demonstrated the most skill. No luck is involved.

People usually tend to believe that contests are more legitimate, as they have to pay the entry fee. One reason that companies like contests so much is that it is another way of generating very affordable advertising. Not only does the contest itself increase consumer interest, but the company might even end up with a catchy slogan or jingle for their product when the contest is over. This slogan might be just as good as one created by a professional marketing firm, and the prize they give to the winner is likely to be less expensive than the exorbitant cost of hiring such a firm.

Legal and Illegal Promotions

A word of caution is due at this point. Although the sweepstakes and contests described above are usually legitimate and legal, illegal versions of them do exist. Never participate in any illegal sweepstake or contest, as there is no guarantee that you can ever collect your winnings, or even that the sweepstake or contest has any winners at all. Illegal sweepstakes and contests are also fundamentally wrong, and law enforcement agencies spend millions of dollars every year trying to put an end to them. So don't make their job more difficult than it already is.

Likewise, lotteries are only legal when run by governments at the state level. No other government, private corporation, or individual may hold a lottery in this country. So if you run into one that is not orchestrated by a state government, then you are advised to steer clear of it, and perhaps even to report it to the police. It is unlikely that you will ever encounter an individual, corporation, or government holding an illegal lottery, as such events usually garner huge amounts of attention and publicity, but in the past confidence tricksters have been known to attempt virtually any scam.

One truly important legal matter to be aware of is that some states prohibit sweepstakes and contests -- we've all heard the phrase "void where prohibited by law." Many people have actually been lucky winners in the past, but were never able to collect their winnings simply because of the state in which they lived. These states still refuse to allow sweepstakes and contests (also known as "promotions") within their borders because of the horrible corruption that surrounded them at one time.

Until the early 1900s, individuals were actually allowed to hold lotteries, but no one ever seemed to win them. Corporations promised even bigger prizes than they do now, but none were ever awarded (and participants were forced to buy products, even though they shouldn't have been). As a result, laws governing promotions became very strict, and some states are still wary of them. So if you live in one of the few states where promotions are prohibited, then try not to be bitter about it. The people who made the laws had your best interests in mind, and they weren't trying to stop you from having fun.

How can you find out if promotions are illegal in your state? This is your second homework assignment. Chances are, if you've never received a promotion mailing at your house before, then you probably live in a state where they are illegal. At one time, corporations that held sweepstakes and contests would send out their mailings indiscriminately, but this resulted in some fairly lengthy legal battles with state governments in which promotions were not permitted. Rather than go through that again, many corporations now simply avoid sending mailings to these states.

But even if you do receive the mailings, this does not automatically mean that promotions are legal in your state. You should go to the local library and look up your state's definitions of legal and illegal gambling in the law books. If you have had no experience trying to interpret such legalese, however, it would probably be even easier to write a letter to a member of your state government. Legislators' addresses can always be found at your local post office, and if you happen to write to one who doesn't know whether or not promotions are legal in your state, then he or she will surely pass on your letter to someone who does know. Finally, the rules that are printed with most sweepstakes and contests usually indicate clearly which states prohibit such a promotion.

Now that you are aware of certain basic features of promotions, we are ready to move on to helping you choose which type of sweepstake or contest is best for you. The following sections of the book will go into various promotions in great depth, including the strategies that may help you become a winner!

SWEEPSTAKES:
GAMES OF PURE LUCK?

CHAPTER 1:
THE NAME OF THE GAME

Make no mistake about it, sweepstakes are games of luck. But you would be amazed at how much luck can be eliminated in your quest to win such a promotion. By reading this book carefully, you will be able to avoid most of the silly mistakes that immediately disqualify up to 90% of your competitors! Imagine how much less you will need to rely on luck if you don't make any of those mistakes.

Anybody can win a sweepstake; no special skills are required. Unlike a contest, you don't have to have a way with words or a particular ability. This is why the people who have won sweepstakes have come from such diverse backgrounds. Rich people, poor people, college graduates, high school dropouts, men, women, young people, and old people have all been winners. Therefore, theoretically speaking, everyone has exactly the same chance of winning.

But do they really? Not exactly. Before your heart sinks, let me reassure you that it's a good thing that not everyone has an equal chance. You see, the odds are not made unequal due to any kind of natural bias inherent to sweepstakes; the odds are made unequal by people who know how to play smart (which is true of just about anything in life, when you think about it). And by the time you put this book down, you'll know how to play smart.

As I mentioned earlier, companies look at sweepstakes as a form of advertisement. As a result, they usually only send entry forms to people whom they believe are most likely to buy their products. Although they cannot force an entrant to buy anything, they certainly hope that people will purchase some of the advertised products. Therefore, if you don't fit into the demographics of a company holding a direct-mail sweepstakes, then there is very little chance that you will be able to enter. If you are sent more than one entry form, however, you can enter as many times as you receive forms. Incidentally, the demographics of different sweepstakes vary greatly. Some companies send entry forms all over the country, and even advertise their sweepstake on the television. Others, such as certain credit card companies, only send their forms to a very select number of people.

Another factor that could prevent you from entering a particular sweepstake is the fact that employees of the company running the game, or of the judging organization, are usually prohibited from entering. This prohibition usually extends to relatives of employees as well.

After you enter a sweepstake, your work is pretty much done. But the company's work has just begun. The winners of most sweep-stakes are picked through random draw-ings. There are usually several drawings, as too many people enter for all the entry forms to fit into one bag or drum. Several entry forms are usually picked by a blind-folded person from each mail sack that the company receives, and then these forms are put into a barrel. Another blindfolded person picks the winners from these forms. Some sweepstakes now assign each entrant a number which is entered into a computer upon receipt of the entry form. The computer then randomly selects the winning numbers.

Almost all companies use independent judging organizations to be responsible for picking the winners. This makes some people very nervous; they think that the judges can get away with giving the prizes to friends and relatives. But rest assured, this never happens. Such organizations are highly reputable firms, and if they were caught cheating in a sweepstake, the repercussions would be too terrible for them to bear.

Surprisingly, many of the prizes in sweepstakes are never claimed by their winners. This is especially strange as all winners are notified in the mail of the prizes they have won. But when a prize goes unclaimed, it does not mean that the company keeps them. Some skeptics think that the company keeps the unclaimed prizes for itself, but this is not true. It would be illegal to do so. They hold new drawings until all the prizes have been given away. This dramatically increases your chances of being a winner.

You can always write to the company that holds the sweepstake for a list of the winners. They will often ask you to enclose a self-addressed-stamped-envelope. If participating in sweepstakes becomes your hobby, then it is a good idea to get into the habit of sending away for such lists; after all, you may have won a prize, but your notification letter could have gotten lost in the mail. It can take several months to receive such a list, however, due to the volume of correspondence a company usually receives after holding a sweepstake or contest.

CHAPTER 2:
DO I NEED AN INVITATION?

There are essentially two types of sweep-stakes. The first, which I have already touched upon, is the direct-mail sweepstake. This is the type of promotion in which you are invited to enter. A com-pany, hoping to advertise its products to you in new and exciting ways, will send you an entry form in the mail. The compa-nies that run this type of promotion have usually done a lot of research on the type of people who buy their products, so they are very particular about who they send an entry form to. This is an unfortunate fact of life when dealing with direct-mail sweep-stakes, and you will probably have to resign yourself to the fact that you cannot enter them all.

The second type of sweepstake is one in which you don't need an invitation to enter. Such a sweepstake is usually advertised in the newspaper or on the container of a product you may have bought (for ex-ample, on the back of a cereal box). This type of sweepstake will usually ask you to send in your name and address on a card. Sometimes you will be asked to send in a proof of purchase, or even just the name of the product written down on the card as well. You can enter this type of sweepstake as often as you like, but be sure to read the rules. Some companies specify that you may not send more than one entry in the same envelope or package.

While we are on the subject of rules (a very important subject indeed!), I would like to remind you to read them very carefully. I will come back to this point shortly. The rules for a direct-mail sweepstake are always enclosed with the entry form. The rules for the second type of sweepstake will always be printed somewhere in the news-paper ad or on the product box.

CHAPTER 3:
RULES AND REGULATIONS

Every promotion that you will ever enter in your entire life will have its own specific set of rules. Don't ever think that you know enough about sweepstakes to stop reading the rules! You are sure to make silly mistakes by doing this. If there is one section of this book that you should basically memorize, then this is definitely it.

Rules, like all fine print, can sometimes be difficult to understand. It would obviously be impossible for me to explain every set of rules to you, so instead I've analyzed the rules of several sweepstakes and compiled all that information into a set of generic guidelines. Most rules you will encounter for sweepstakes will be very similar, so after reading over this section one or two times, you should be able to understand any set of rules and regulations without too much difficulty at all.

In order to make this example as realistic as possible, I have created the name of a corporation that does not exist as the company running the sweepstake, and I have also made up the date of the deadline for entry.

RULE 1. *Greetings from the Yummy-Yum Candy Corporation. To enter our fabulous new sweepstake, you may either use our official entry blank, or you can use a 3-by-5 inch plain piece of paper.*

Most sweepstakes print official entry cards, but they often say you can substitute the card with a piece of paper of a specific size. This size is usually 3-by-5 inch. Promotions are usually very specific about what you can use as a substitute for the entry blank; some say a piece of paper, some say an index card. Always be sure to use the correct substitute. Furthermore, some promotions, such as the example given above, say the piece of paper (or card, in other promotions) must be plain. That means *no* lines.

It would probably be a good idea for you to go to the store and buy a variety of different size cards and papers, some lined and some unlined, so that you are prepared to enter any sweepstake that comes your way.

Never send your entry in on a post card unless the rules specifically state that this is an acceptable substitute for the entry blank. Moreover, never photocopy the entry blank unless the rules indicate you may do so. Each year judges throw out hundreds of entries that could have been winners, because the entrant assumed it would be okay to use a photocopy of the entry form.

RULE 2. *Hand-print your name and address on the entry blank, or on the piece of paper. Print in block letters.*

This rule means that you should not type the entry card. Only type it if the rules specifically say that you can do so. It also means that you cannot hand-write it in cursive. This rule says to hand-*print* your information in block letters, so that is what you should do. Block letters are large, *capital* letters that are easy to read.

Always print your full name. Do not use any aliases or nicknames, as winners are usually required to furnish proof of identification. Always print your full address, including your apartment number and zip code. Small mistakes such as this could cost you thousands of dollars.

RULE 3. *Send your entry in a hand-printed envelope.*

Again, hand-print the company's address as well as your return address. Do not type or write in cursive unless they indicate that you may do so. Do not adorn the envelope with fancy labels or stickers. Be sure to print the sweepstake company's address exactly as it appears in the rules. If you find several sweepstake company addresses in the rules, then use any of them. Sometimes companies give several addresses and monitor the quantity of mail they receive at each address; this has no effect on the outcome of the sweepstake, but it allows them to analyze if certain type-faces in their advertisements attract a reader's attention better than others.

Unless otherwise indicated, you may not use an envelope that is larger than a #10 envelope. This is the long, white business envelope. You may usually use a smaller envelope if you wish, but experienced entrants of promotion tend to prefer the #10 size.

RULE 4. *Enclose the wrapper from a Yummy-Yum Deluxe Bon-Bon with your entry, or hand-print in block letters the words "Yummy-Yum Deluxe Bon-Bon" on a separate 3-by-5 inch plain piece of paper.*

As this is a sweepstake, the company cannot demand that you buy their product. Therefore you do not have to enclose a wrapper. If you choose to print the words, again remember that you may not type or write in cursive unless the rules specifically allow you to do so. The quotation marks surrounding the words may or may not be necessary, but put them in just in case (unless the rules say that you shouldn't). Note that this promotion's rules indicate to print the words on a separate piece of paper. Some will ask you to print them on the same piece of paper with your name and address. Be sure to follow this rule carefully. Moreover, if the rules indicate to print the words on a separate piece of paper, do not attach it to the piece of paper with your name and address unless the rules tell you to. If they want the two pieces of paper attached, then they will usually be very specific about how you should attach them.

RULE 5. *Enter as often as you wish, but mail all entries separately. All entries must be received by February 8, 2025.*

If the rules allow you to enter as many times as you want, then be sure to do so. If you plan to enter many times, then you will soon realize how handy it is to have a supply of various index cards and pieces of paper on hand. Don't worry about entering too often; even if a judge sees your name a million times, he or she cannot throw any eligible entry away. There is no such thing as promotion "blacklisting." That would be illegal.

You must mail your entries separately. There is no use in sending in ten-thousand entries if you pack them in the same envelope or box, because they will all be disqualified. This means that you may have to spend quite a bit on postage, but you cannot get away with breaking the rules. This rule indicates that entries must be received by February 8, 2025. If a rule is phrased in such a way, then it is a good idea to mail your entry no later than two or three days before the date given; this gives you some time if there is any delay in the mail. Some rules say that entries must be post marked by a certain date; that means that you can wait until that very day to put your entry in the mailbox, as the post office will post mark your envelope later that day.

RULE 6. *Winners are determined by a random drawing.*

This means exactly what it says. Certain sweepstakes may indicate that winners are determined randomly by computer.

RULE 7. *No substitutions will be made in awarding prizes. Only one prize per household. All prizes will be awarded.*

Sweepstakes almost never let you choose the prize you win. Therefore, only enter the sweepstakes that offer things you might like to have. It would be horrible if you won a big, ugly piece of furniture that didn't match any of your other furniture. It might even be so ugly that you can't sell it, and your victory would turn out to be a wasted experience. Sometimes incomplete prizes are even offered. For example, they may offer a vacation, but not pay the airfare. Is this really the kind of prize you want?

Usually, only one prize is awarded per household. This means that if three unrelated people who all live at exactly the same address all win prizes in the same sweepstake, only one will be allowed to collect his or her prize. If this ever happens, the company may disqualify all three entrants. If a single individual wins more than one prize, then the company has the right to choose which prize that person gets to keep. Some rules specify that only one prize is allowed per family, rather than per household.

The rules usually indicate that all prizes will be awarded. As I mentioned earlier, this means that the judges will continue to hold drawings until all the prizes have been given away.

RULE 8. *Winning odds are determined by the number of entries received.*

The more eligible entries the sweepstake receives, the smaller your chance of winning.

RULE 9. *Winners must take all responsibility for local, state, and federal taxes on their prizes.*

Occasionally (but very rarely) a sweepstake will pay the taxes for the winners. Taxation of winnings will be discussed in more detail in a later chapter, but it is important to mention it here. Remember that ugly piece of furniture you won? You still have to pay taxes on it, even if you can't sell it to anyone, so you could actually end up losing money.

RULE 10. *Sweepstakes are open to the residents of the continental United Sates. Entrants must be at least 18 years of age. Employees and families of the employees of the Yummy-Yum Candy Corporation, the independent judging firm, and the advertising agency are not eligible. Void where prohibited.*

These are the final eligibility requirements for winning a prize. Even if you have done everything else correctly, if you don't meet these requirements, you will not receive a prize. And companies that sponsor sweepstakes are very careful to make sure that these requirements are met, so don't even bother trying to lie.

Note that this rule indicates that the sweepstake is only open to residents of the continental U.S. If you live in Alaska, you're out of luck. If you live in Hawaii, you're out of luck. If you live in Puerto Rico, you're out of luck. The geographic requirements of different sweepstakes sometimes vary greatly, so be sure to read this rule carefully.
This sweepstake requires you to be at least 18 years old. Some say that you must be at least 16, and some say at least 21. Again, double-check to make sure you qualify.

If you work for any of the companies listed in the rules, or if *anyone* in your family (even your crazy Great Uncle Harry, whom no one likes to admit is a part of the family) works for any of the companies, then you're out of luck. Sorry, but that's the way it is.

And by now we all know what "void where prohibited" means.

That's a pretty complete set of rules. If you can understand them, then you should be able to understand the rules to any promotion. And if you can understand the rules, then you can be sure not to make the simple mistakes that eliminate as many as 90% of the entrants! Don't you feel like your chances of winning are better already?

CHAPTER 4:
WHEN WILL OPPORTUNITY KNOCK?

We've all heard the quote, "Luck is where preparation meets opportunity." Unfortunately, we usually hear this quote when we are feeling unlucky (take, for example, the time when the biggest jerk in the office got the promotion *you* were expecting). But now that you are well versed in the general rules for sweepstakes, you should feel much more prepared to enter. So when will opportunity knock? When will you get the chance to turn your preparation into luck?

Never!

Let me repeat myself: never! Opportunity won't knock on your door. You have to go out and seek opportunity for yourself. In other words, you have to make your own breaks in life. This is true of just about everything else in life, so why shouldn't it be true of sweepstakes? Remember, to become proficient at a hobby, you must dedicate much of your free time to it.

So where do you go in order to find opportunity? Where can you go to find all the sweepstakes? If you don't know the answer to this question, then you should be glad! Because if you don't know, then that means most other people don't know either. The fact is, companies across the country usually hold *thousands* of sweepstakes every year, but most people miss out on them because they just don't know where to look. But if you look in the places listed below, then you will probably discover that there are far too many sweepstakes to enter them all.

The first place you should check each week is in newspapers and magazines. The most effective medium in which to advertise today is certainly television, but many companies cannot afford to advertise all of their promotions on TV due to the high cost of air time. As a result, they advertise heavily in newspapers and magazines, where ad space is much cheaper. National magazines such as *Reader's Digest* are a veritable gold mine of sweepstakes.

If you are ever to be a serious sweepstaker, then you must subscribe to at least one national magazine; you may want to try subscribing to more than one, but you might find that exactly the same promotions are advertised in each. Other magazines that frequently contain advertisements for promotions are *TV Guide*, *Family Circle*, and *Ladies' Home Journal*. Remember, although companies cannot force you to buy anything in order to enter a sweepstake, they certainly hope that you will buy their products. As a result, companies try to advertise in magazines that are read by the people whom they think will buy their products. Moreover, the prizes given away in sweepstakes sometimes reflect the kind of products that the company sells. Therefore, if you are interested in winning a car or other automotive products, then you might want to flip through a car magazine every now and then. If you want a house or home furnishings, then take a look at several home decorating magazines. You might even find it possible to combine two separate hobbies in this way, which could be a very rewarding experience.

Since subscribing to magazines can become

expensive, you might want to take regular trips to the local library. In consideration of everyone else, you shouldn't rip out any entry forms that you find in magazines or newspapers there, but you can at least copy down addresses and complete rules for each sweepstake. If you are creative, you will be able to think of even more places to find magazines. What about while you're waiting in your dentist's office? Or what about at your friends' houses?

Don't limit yourself to national magazines. Although there are more cases of fraud in sweepstakes advertised in local newspapers and magazines, most of them are still very legitimate. And if you like the prizes that some of them offer, don't be afraid to enter them. The most that you have to lose is five minutes of your time, a piece of paper (or two), an envelope, and a postage stamp. The one thing that should never stop you from entering a sweepstake is your fear that it will not be judged honestly; the invest-ment is always very small, and the potential rewards are always very great.

The second place where you should always look is in your local supermarket and other shops. Since many companies that run sweepstakes make products found in grocery stores and other shops, it is only natural that they should advertise their promotions in these stores.

It is usually very easy to find sweepstake notices, as well as their entry blanks, in these stores. Most companies specifically ask store managers to place them in a location where they are likely to be seen by customers. Most often they can be found on the shelves right next to the products that the company sells. They are also often located near the checkout stands, where people are liable to take note of them while waiting to pay for their goods. Occasionally, some stores have special bulletin boards on which you can find notices for promotions. You may wish to ask the store manager about such a board.

If you can't find any entry blanks alongside the sweepstake notices, don't hesitate to ask the store manager about them. Sometimes experienced sweepstakers have already grabbed all the entry blanks, but the managers make sure to keep some extra ones in their office. And sometimes the manager simply forgets to place the entry blanks in the storefront. If you absolutely cannot track down any entry blanks, then take a few minutes to read the rules on the sweepstake notice. Perhaps the rules will give an address where you can write for a blank. Or perhaps, as with most sweepstakes, you can simply enter the promotion with an index card or piece of paper.

Your third option for locating sweepstakes is probably the most enjoyable, but it certainly requires the most time. Many experienced sweepstakers across the country are forming sweepstake and contest clubs. These clubs are a wonderful way of networking information about promotions; you can share information and entry blanks with your friends. By joining such a club, you not only limit the amount of work you have to do (rather than check every grocery store in town, you only have to check one, because other people in the club are responsible for other stores), but you can also build some lasting friendships. Some of these clubs have grown to such large memberships that they now actually hold national conventions. Many of them also publish widely read newsletters, filled with tips to improve your chances of winning. If you do a little research at your local library, you should be able to determine whether or not such a club already exists in your town. If a club does not yet exist, then you can form one yourself. All it takes is a little initiative!

In order to figure out which of these three suggestions is best for you, you have to ask yourself a few questions. The first, and most important, question is whether or not you want the prizes offered by certain sweepstakes. For example, if you know that you want furniture, don't bother going to stores which seem to advertise sweepstakes specializing in clothing. Remember, a sweepstake isn't worth entering if you wouldn't *buy* the prizes. As will be discussed later in this book, unwanted prizes can sometimes be surprisingly difficult to get rid of; many "unlucky" winners have received prizes that they did not want, and were unable to sell, but they still had to pay taxes on them. Imagine losing money by winning a promotion! You obviously would not want to ruin the joy of winning a sweepstake by winning something you don't like. If the prizes that you desire are very specific, then you might want to consider either of the first two options (doing research in newspapers and magazines, and going to the *appropriate* stores). But keep in mind that if you become too selective of the promotions that you choose to enter, then you will decrease your overall chances of winning. After all, the more promotions you enter, the greater the odds of your victory. As an experienced sweepstaker, you will walk a fine line; you must find a comfortable balance between entering as many promotions as possible, and entering only those that interest you the most.

The second question to ask yourself is how much time you wish to devote to your new hobby. If you truly enjoy sweepstaking, and you are willing to give it a high priority in

47

your precious free time, then you might want to join a sweepstake club. That way your hobby can become an even more enriching experience by meeting others who share your love for it. If this is the way in which you choose to pursue sweepstaking, then it really doesn't matter whether or not you are very selective in what kinds of prizes you want to win. In the club that you join (or start), you are bound to find people whose tastes are very selective, as well as people who would enjoy winning any prizes. In other words, clubs are made up of all kinds of people, and you will most likely meet someone who shares your interests exactly.

The third question to ask yourself is which one of the three suggestions will give you the greatest chances of winning. Perhaps you are not interested in spending too much time on your new hobby, but you know of a local club. You should at least give the club a chance, because you might meet one or two people with whom you could network, thereby dramatically in-creasing your chances of winning without taking up too much of your time.

CHAPTER 5:
HOW TO BE A WINNER!

By this time, I am sure that you have realized that there are no sure fire ways to win a sweepstake. This book is designed to help you maximize your potential for winning, so that you won't let any opportunity pass you by. But there are certain hints that you may find useful. Perhaps, after reading this chapter, you will have discovered a helpful hint that I have overlooked. By all means write it down immediately, as you might forget it later. It would probably even be useful to write it in the margins of this book, so that you can keep all of your information regarding sweepstakes in one place.

HINT 1. *Mail to more than one address.*

Earlier in this book I mentioned that sweepstake notices sometimes list several addresses. As you now know, this is simply a monitoring device employed by the company to determine which aspect of its advertising is most effective. You can use these addresses to your advantage by mailing entries to each of them (so long as the rules indicate you may enter more than once). This way, your entry has a chance of being picked out of several mail sacks, giving you better odds of being the final winner.

HINT 2. *Don't send all of your entries in on the same day.*

Much like sending entries to all the addresses, doing this spreads your blanks out. You can guarantee yourself that you have entries in several mail sacks. While having 100 entries in one mail sack certainly increases your chance of being picked, having 100 entries each in three mail sacks increases it three times more.

HINT 3. *Send in your entries as close to the deadline as possible.*

Although the judges are careful never to skip over any mail sacks, the entries that they pick out of the last sack will naturally be at the top of the barrel when they do the final drawing. Therefore, it is probably best for you to send in all of your entries during the final week before the deadline passes.

HINT 4. *Find ways to save time for yourself.*

You will soon discover that filling out hundreds of entry blanks can take up hours of your time. If the rules for any sweepstake allow you to photocopy your entries, then by all means do so (but, be warned, very few allow this). Abbreviate anything that will not be confusing to the judges; for example, write "St" rather than "Street." But never abbreviate anything that could raise a question in the judges' minds, or you will probably be disqualified. For example, never abbreviate the name of the product, and never shorten your own name.

HINT 5. *Break down the entry process into a number of steps, and then perform each step in large groups.*

What I mean by this is that you should not write out your entry blank, then put it in the envelope, then write the address on the envelope, then seal the envelope, then attach the stamp to it, and then finally move on the next entry. Doing one step at a time like this is fine if you are just sending out one letter, but when mailing things in bulk it becomes very slow. First, you should fill out all of your entry blanks, index cards, or pieces of paper. Then you should address all of your envelopes. Then you should stamp all of your envelopes. Then you should place the entries in all of your envelopes. Then, finally, seal all of your envelopes. Working in stages like this is the only way to perform such tasks without driving yourself crazy. Moreover, by dividing the process up into several jobs, you might be able to get people to help you.

HINT 6. *Only enter the promotions which you are really interested in winning.*

If you do your research thoroughly, you will find that there are far too many sweepstakes for you to enter them all, so only enter the ones you really like. As I said earlier, a certain amount of selectivity will come with experience. I am sure that most of the promotions that you enter will be the larger, national ones, but don't forget about the local ones altogether.

HINT 7. *Remember to check if promotions are legal in your state, that you are old enough to enter, and that you meet all other eligibility requirements.*

If you don't, then don't even waste your time entering. If promotions are illegal in your state, then don't get upset about it. It's just an annoying fact of life. But you might at least want to write to your state legislators about this. If they receive enough letters, then they could seriously consider revising the laws regarding gaming in their state.

CONTESTS:
GAMES OF SKILL

CHAPTER 6:
THE NAME IS THE GAME

Contests absolutely require more skill than sweepstakes do. There are several types of contests, but most require the contestant to write a rhyme or a slogan. Many, but not all, contests require a proof of purchase from a product.

Companies are sometimes reluctant to sponsor contests, usually opting in favor of sweepstakes, for several reasons. In the past, companies have run into legal problems, and they have had to state in a court of law why they felt one slogan was better than another. While this is a very rare occurrence, and to my knowledge neither a company nor its judging organization has ever lost such a court battle, contests always result in many disgruntled people who honestly feel that they provided the best entry. In fact, companies are inevitably swamped by letters from these people, demanding an explanation for their loss; as you can imagine, this is not the kind of positive advertising that a company hopes to generate by holding a promotion. Moreover, contests usually fail to attract a large number of entrants, as many people feel they do not possess the talent needed to win.

But contests are becoming more common. The reasons for this are simple. Firstly, whereas sweepstakes have been opposed at various times by local and federal legislators, people rarely have any suspicions about a contest due to the fact that skill is required. And secondly, a really good entry in a contest could result in a very successful ad campaign for a company; rather than pay experts hundreds of thousands of dollars to come up with a catchy slogan, why not ask you to do it?

People often get upset when they discover that they have to purchase a product in order to enter, but this is quite silly. How could you ever write a jingle or a slogan if you have never even used the product? The judges can usually tell which contestants are truly familiar with the product, and they immediately disqualify those that are not; in fact, contests often stipulate that sincerity is one of the qualities that the judges look for when selecting the best entry. If this seems unfair to you in any way, it shouldn't. After all, companies are looking for a contestant who can paint the smallest details of a product in the most appealing light. For example, a company that makes dish washing detergent wants you to describe how effortlessly their product works and how wonderful it smells, not just that it cleans dishes.

As with sweepstakes, a list of the contest's winners is available upon demand, usually several months after the contest is over. But don't ask the company to send you a copy of the winning slogan, because they will absolutely refuse to do so. You may wish to see the winning entry so that you can get a better idea of what contest sponsors look for in a slogan or a jingle, but you must remember that the judges have to make subjective decisions. Contest writing is a creative process, not a science, and as a result some entries will simply appeal to the judges more than others. Companies realize this, and they do not want to alienate you by revealing a winning entry that you feel is inferior to your own.

It is worthwhile to point out that being a serious contestant requires a tremendous amount of devotion on your part. Don't just think you can whip out a catchy phrase after a few short minutes behind the typewriter. If it were that simple, then advertising agencies would not have multi-million dollar contracts with corporations. You must practice your skills at every possible moment, occupying your spare time by trying to invent new jingles for the products you use. But don't be scared by the amount of effort you must exert; I cannot tell you how fulfilling it is to write a catchy phrase or create a new tune. As with all things in life, the contests that take the most time are also the most rewarding!

CHAPTER 7:
FROM RHYMES TO RECIPES

There are two major types of contests. Firstly, there are word contests, which ask you to create a rhyme, a slogan, a jingle, a caption, or to explain why you use a certain product in twenty five words or less. Secondly, there are recipe and cooking contests, in which you are asked to create simple yet delicious culinary delights.

The best thing about the word contests is that the sponsor usually indicates what criteria the judges use to rate an entry. Again, as contests help the sponsor with advertising, they want you to do the best writing that you can; they do not want to trick you or prevent you from creating a masterpiece. So if a word contest's rules say that you should stress "clarity, originality, sincerity, and aptness of thought," then you should be clear, original, sincere, and apt of thought.

Very few winning entries ever actually become ad slogans (which is one of the reasons why contests are not as common as sweepstakes), but some have been incredibly successful. About a decade ago, a deodorant company ran a contest, and their winning entry became the slogan behind one of the most successful advertisement campaigns of all time.

The key to being a successful word contester is to follow the old "SOS rule." This rule means: be Simple, be Original, and be Sincere. Techniques for achieving these qualities will be discussed in a later chapter of this book. And always remember to follow the rules!

Recipe contests are the second major type of contest. They have one distinct advantage over word contests: you don't need to learn a new skill in order to participate. Whereas most of you are probably not writers, almost all of you have spent time in the kitchen. You all have secret family recipes handed down to you from your parents and grandparents. Chances are there is at least one dish that you prepare every so often, perhaps when you have guests over, that drives everyone wild! Who knows, this dish could win you thousands of dollars.

I want to stress at this point that recipe contests are not the sole domain of women. More and more men are beginning to enter the kitchen, and many are discovering a remarkable talent for concocting delicious meals. Historically, many of the big winners of cooking contests have been women, but recently men have made some startling victories. So, if you are a man, don't think that you have to skip this section of the book.

Although I will discuss specific strategies to help you with cooking contests later in this book, I would like to give you a few hints now. In advertising, presentation is at least as important as content. Since contests are a form of advertising, this rule holds true. Even if you have a delicious new recipe, you might not get very far if you don't present it well to the judges. You have to send in a recipe that looks and sounds so delicious that it will make the judges' mouths water just by reading it.

You are probably thinking that you should try to make recipes that the judges will want to eat themselves, and you are right. The problem is trying to figure out what they want to eat. It is obviously impossible to predict what flavors someone enjoys, so the best thing for you to do is research what kinds of dishes have won contests recently. In order to do this, you will probably have to subscribe to a national magazine such as *Family Circle*, which regularly publishes winning recipes. Compare the ingredients from each. Compare the methods of cooking and the necessary preparation time. Look for similarities. There aren't that many independent judging organizations in this country, so it is only natural that the same people often judge many contests. Therefore, with a little research, you should be able to find some clues as to what will be well received.

But this is not to say that you should merely copy another recipe, or simply make a slight variation on it, because this will result in your immediate disqualification. Originality is just as important in cooking as it is in word contests. With recipes, you should always follow the old "SO rule:" be

Simple, but be Original. You need to present a dish that is easy to make, uses inexpensive ingredients that are easy to find, and tastes delicious. And don't forget, you need to present it with some flare.

CHAPTER 8:
SOS / SO

The rules for most word contests specify that your entry will be judged for its aptness of thought, originality, sincerity, and clarity. Moreover, the rules usually indicate, in percentages, how much attention will be paid to each of these traits; sincerity, for example, is often rated over twenty five percent. But what exactly does this mean, and how can you tailor your entry to stress these qualities? That's what this chapter is all about.

Aptness, or appropriateness, is important because the company sponsoring the contest wants to find out what you specifically like about the product. Therefore, your entry must be highly specific, suggesting particular qualities of the product you are writing about. In other words, if your entry describes toothpaste just as aptly as it describes self-sealing tires, then chances are it won't win. It is also important to remember that you are trying to endorse a specific company's product. Don't just rattle on about why brushing with fluoride toothpaste is important. Instead, clearly indicate why brushing your teeth with "Bright-n-Shiny" brand toothpaste is important.

There is a very good chance that you will never have used some of the products that you hope to write about, and you cannot simply try to write about them without knowing their virtues. As a result, if you don't already own the product, you will have to invest some of your hard-earned money in buying it for each contest you wish to enter. I realize that this may initially seem like a terrible thing to have to do, but remember that you are required to devote a certain amount of time and money to any hobby if you wish to succeed at it. If you are going to enter a contest for "Bright-n-Shiny" fluoride toothpaste, go out and buy a tube. Brush your teeth with it. What does it taste like? Does it leave more or less grit in your mouth than your regular brand does? What color is it? How does it smell? Does it lather up a lot or a little? You *must* know these things. And you never know, you may even discover that you actually like this brand better.

When advertisers try to market a product, they make lists of qualities known as sales points. For example, a sales point of

"Bright-n-Shiny" might be that it tastes better than another leading fluoride toothpaste. So when you sit down to enter a contest, you might want to approach it by listing the sales points. This can be quite a time consuming process, and it raises an interesting point; you will be able to complete such a list more quickly, and therefore enter more contests, if you write about things with which you are somewhat familiar. Thus, if you know absolutely nothing about lawn care, and are not really interested in learning anything about it, then you may want to steer clear of contests for gardening products.

I will return to sincerity, originality, and clarity (simplicity) later in this chapter, but for now I would like to discuss ways in which you can apply your aptness of thought. In other words, how you should describe the sponsor's product.

Any successful writer needs a variety of reference books. This is true for the greatest of artists, such as Shakespeare, as well as for the contest entrant. I could not even have written this book without my own personal reference library. But what constitutes a library? Many scholars equip themselves with *The Oxford English Dictionary*, a tremendous volume (usually sold on computer disk now) that not only defines words, but also places them in the context of great works of art. *The Oxford English Dictionary*'s entry for the word tragedy, for example, makes reference to Shakespeare's *Romeo and Juliet*. These scholars are also sure to have on hand a dictionary of synonyms and antonyms, so that they can expand their comprehension of various words. Many also like to have a reputable encyclopedia, a rhyming dictionary, and a book of quotations.

But do you need all that? Of course not. All you need is a good dictionary and a good thesaurus. You can usually buy both of them in a set for about twenty or thirty dollars, and they are well worth the expense. Don't buy the small paperback copies, as they are not very thorough. Do yourself the favor of investing in the large hard cover copies.

You should use the dictionary as a foundation for your writing. Refer to it whenever you have questions about spelling and questions about usage. But also refer to it throughout the process of making the list of sales points. You may be able to find several meanings for some of the words you put on the list, which will allow you to make a pun in your slogan (which judges often seem to like). The large hard cover dictionaries sometimes include antonyms as well, enabling you to contrast your words with their opposites. The thesaurus will also come in handy while making the list, as you will find many synonyms which will give your writing the flare it needs to win.

Once you have these books, you will be able to use language to its full advantage. But I cannot stress enough the fact that the key to being a successful writer is practice, practice, practice. No books on your shelves, no fancy word processors, no hints that I can give you will be of any use if you don't practice your skills. Think of anyone you have ever seen who is incredibly skillful: a basketball player, a race car driver, an archer, a poet, a physicist. One of the reasons that they seem to achieve their goals so effortlessly is that they have spent countless hours practicing.

In order to communicate effectively in your entry, you must have something to say. But you must also say it with style. If you can do this (which you will find challenging, even after reading this book and practicing), then you stand a good chance of winning. But how can you develop a style of your own? By following some of the suggestions below, you should be able to write with considerable pizzazz. Incidentally, this list of suggestions is by no means exhaustive, so if you can think of any that I have forgotten, then do not hesitate to add them.

1. COMPARISONS. There are two types of comparisons that you can make between things. The first is the *simile*. Similes compare two things by using the words "like" or "as." For example, "Her tears fell like rain" is a simile. The second type is the

metaphor. Metaphors are considered slightly more sophisticated than similes because they dispense with "like" or "as" and simply imply the comparison. An example of this could be, "The race car driver was a bird of prey."

The strength of metaphors is illustrated even in this example. By omitting "like" or "as", it adds intensity to the sentence. You can really imagine the race car driver swooping around the track, desperately trying to catch up with and overtake all of his opponents, hungering to win the grand prize. Try reading the example again, but this time include the word "like." You see? It loses much of its force. For this reason, judges tend to prefer metaphors to similes.

Metaphors have an added advantage in that they can more easily convey action than similes, which is another thing that attracts judges. For example, in the previous paragraph I wrote, "You can really imagine the race car driver *swooping* around the track." This is also a metaphor, as it implies a connection between the driver and the bird. And a final advantage is that they are slightly shorter. When asked to describe why you love "Bright-n-Shiny" toothpaste in twenty five words or less, a single word could be crucial.

2. PERSONIFICATION. Personification is a special type of metaphor in which inanimate objects are compared to living creatures, usually people. Thus "The race car *driver* swooped around the track" is not personification, but "The race car swooped around the track" is. This is possibly the single most important language technique that you will use in your entries. You will probably be able to use it in every single contest you enter. You can describe how a stain remover works by writing "Cleano stain remover eats stains away." You can describe the toothpaste by writing "Bright-n-Shiny brushes plaque away." And if you look carefully at advertisements from now on, I am sure that you will discover that professional ad campaigns rely heavily on personification. Think how many times you have seen talking bubbles or maple syrup jugs on TV commercials.

3. ALLITERATION. This is a technique in which many of the words in a sentence start with the same letter (technically, if the letter is a vowel then it is called assonance, and if the letter is a consonant then it is called consonance). Judges are also generally attracted to this. You have to be very careful with this technique, however, as it so easily begins to sound dumb. If you write, "Poker brand Popsicles pack a powerful yet pleasing punch," then you are bound to annoy the judges. Subtlety is the key! Try to limit your alliteration to three or four words, and if you intersperse them throughout a sentence, then you could give your entry a pleasing ring that will delight the judges.

4. TYPOS. Typos (those done on purpose, that is) can also be amusing. If you can somehow work such a technique into your entry, then it could help you be a winner. If you are entering a contest sponsored by Luscious brand snack foods, then you might want to declare their cupcakes "De-Luscious." But, as you can see by this example, you have to be very careful when

using this; it can seem extremely gimmicky. In fact, many judges are so sick of receiving entries with typos that they actually have a grudge against contestants who rely on them. So never use this technique unless you *really* feel it will improve your entry.

5. RHYMES. Although rhymes can be useful in any contest, they tend to work best in jingles. But, as with any other technique, they must be used sparingly. The rules of some contests specifically tell you to avoid rhymes, whereas others encourage it. Rhyming almost always goes hand in hand with meter, or rhythm. If you try to say some rhymes in your head, you will probably notice yourself talking in a sing-song voice. This is another reason why rhyming is usually best saved for jingles.

6. PUNS. This can be a very effective technique of grabbing the judges' attention. Puns allow your entry to have a double meaning, but you must remember to keep such puns simple. Never allude to literary masterpieces that many people haven't read. Never allude to a foreign language,

which is bound to confuse not only the general public but the judges as well.

There are really two types of puns. First, there are implied puns, in which the words in a sentence can be interpreted more than one way. These are the most difficult to achieve, and are therefore often the favorite of judges. Second, there are puns in which you create a variation on a word. These are somewhat easier to make, but they can sometimes be very effective. For example, you might want to advertise a Renaissance Fair using the words "Knight Life."

7. GROUPING. Grouping usually occurs in pairs or triads (groups of three). Although the two have a very similar effect, you construct them in entirely different ways. Pairs generally involve opposites that balance out a phrase. Many years ago a contestant won a fortune with the entry "A winner never quits, and a quitter never wins." As impressive as pairing may seem, triads are even more so. Rather than oppose each other, however, the words in triads sometimes support each other. Take words

from your list of sales points and try to combine them in interesting ways. One famous triad was used as the name of a Clint Eastwood movie in the early 70's: *The Good, The Bad, and the Ugly*. Note that these words seem to work with each other; you'll probably find this technique most effective when combining it with another, such as alliteration. This technique is probably the most difficult one to achieve, so if you have some success with it you should feel very proud of yourself.

Now that you understand the ways in which you can create a style, let us return to the basic rules of simplicity, originality, and sincerity. As I have already stated many times, you must use these techniques as sparingly and simply as possible, or else they will lose their punch and become tiresome. I have already discussed sincerity, or the ability to convincingly praise a certain brand of product through your experience with it. So now we are left with originality.

Judges consider originality to be the ability

to express your ideas in a unique way. All of the techniques you have just read about will certainly help you to be original, but you also need to approach each contest from a new angle. If you are asked to write a slogan for "Bright-n-Shiny" toothpaste, rather than discuss its cavity fighting ability, perhaps you could think about the fresh breath it creates. From there, you can conclude what kind of an effect this will have on a person's romantic life, and come up with the slogan, "Lovers love Bright-n-Shiny toothpaste." Hopefully your entries will be better than that, but you get the idea.

We now move on to recipe contests. Not surprisingly, the judges of these contests also consider originality to be a major factor in their decision. In fact, *most* entries are eliminated immediately because they aren't original; sometimes they are straight ripoffs of old recipes, and other times they are so close to old recipes that they might as well be ripoffs. Remember, your recipe must be significantly different from any other in order to be a contender.

A minor change in the ingredients or their amounts is not different enough. But surprisingly, you can make a recipe that tastes very similar to an old favorite if you have a new, easy way to prepare it. Ease of preparation is an extremely important criterion in cooking contests, often being of equal or greater weight to originality in the judging. Don't think that your dish has to have less than five ingredients in order to be considered easy, however. In fact, many winning dishes have many ingredients, but they are very straightforward. These recipes don't call for any elaborate methods of preparation, such as dicing fish into perfect one inch cubes, sautéing them in butter for just under 52 seconds, and adding two drops of vanilla extract exactly twelve-and-a-half seconds into the procedure. Whenever possible, it is even recommended that you substitute "ready-to-serve" ingredients whenever possible; if your recipe calls for chicken stock, then use stock from a can, rather than slowly boiling a chicken all day long. A good guideline for determining ease of preparation is to ask yourself whether or not you would be willing to make it after coming home from a long day at work.

All recipe contests will stipulate that you use a certain ingredient in your dish. After all, this is a form of advertising for their product. Therefore, if you are entering a contest sponsored by Yummy Yum Chocolates, then they will ask you to use at least one of their candy bars in the recipe. Never use less than the amount they ask you to use! If possible, use even more, as this will impress the judges. In general, winning entries use more than the minimum amount.

Another important factor is cost. Are the ingredients expensive? Contest sponsors usually look for recipes that will appeal to people on a tight budget, so don't bother sending in a delightful way to prepare lobster tail. And don't think that the judges might be interested in trying something new and expensive; they always want to taste something original and different, but they are usually given strict limits by the contest sponsor as to how expensive the dish can be.

There is only one exception to this rule, but in general I would not even recommend this. If your recipe does call for an expensive ingredient, and if there is no cheaper substitute for that ingredient, then you can submit the recipe so long as the leftovers can be saved. If your ingredients must be consumed immediately, then don't bother.

A third factor is the availability of the ingredients. If your recipe calls for an obscure spice that is only cultivated every ninth month in southern China, then don't bother submitting it, no matter how good it tastes. In this sense, availability of the ingredients is related very closely with cost. A good way of insuring availability of ingredients is to shop only at national supermarket chains. This will eliminate the possibility of any items being available only in certain regions of the country. Traditionally, winning recipes have been those in which normal ingredients result in a fabulous taste, and this is one way in which you should never break with tradition. Again, if you buy canned and other already prepared foods, you will help guarantee availability.

There are some recipe contests which call for ethnic foods, but you should try to ensure the availability of ingredients as much as possible even for these promotions. Just because you're making an Italian dish doesn't mean you should have to travel to Italy to find the things you need.

Once you have developed a delicious recipe, however, your work is far from over. In the first place, you have to think about the way to present it. Never forget the garnishing, unless the rules of the contest forbid it (always read the rules!), and always make the dish colorful and rich in texture. The recipe should *look* delicious, not just taste it. But never allow the look to become more important than the taste.

The final step, actually writing up the recipe, will be discussed in the following chapter.

CHAPTER 9:
RULES AND REGULATIONS

While the rules and regulations for contests are far more diverse than those for sweepstakes, there are certain hints that I can give you in order to prevent you from making silly mistakes that result in immediate disqualification. As with sweepstakes, I will provide you with a sample set of rules for a contest, but be warned that any rules you may come across could be *totally* different. This only makes sense when you consider that there are many different types of contests, asking you to perform a variety of skills, whereas all sweepstakes work in essentially the same way. I therefore suggest that you read this chapter very carefully, so that you can analyze all sets of regulations in the same fashion that I do.

RULE 1. *Greetings from the Yummy-Yum Candy Corporation, and good luck with our fabulous new contest! To enter, you must complete the last three lines of this limerick:*
"There once was a Peruvian dandy,
Who loved his Yummy-Yum candy"

You've never heard of a limerick before? Don't panic. Later on in the rules, you will get specific instructions on how to write a limerick, which is a type of poem. Right now you should concentrate on the fact that they asked you to complete *three lines*. That means you must write three more lines; not two, not four! Always do exactly as the rules tell you! You wouldn't believe how many poor contestants are disqualified simply because they thought it would be more creative to write a different number of lines. Usually, a word contest will specify some type of a limit; in many cases you are asked not to exceed twenty five words.

RULE 2. *Using either the official entry blank or a plain piece of 8 1/2 x 11" paper, hand print your name, address, zip code, and complete the limerick. Lines 3 and 4 must rhyme, and line 5 must rhyme with lines 1 and 2.*

Once again you have the choice of using the official blank or your own piece of paper. Note that this piece of paper is a different size than the one indicated in the sweepstake rule, which is why I suggested buying several different types of paper. Note that it says a "plain" piece of paper, meaning unlined. And also note that it does not state that a photocopy of the official blank is acceptable, so don't photocopy it.

These rules tell you to hand print. This means that you should neither type, nor write in cursive. Hand print only! Although it does not specify for you to do so, it would probably be best for you to use block letters. Fill in your full address, including apartment number and zip code, just as the instructions ask you to. This is exactly the same as for sweepstakes.

Finally, the last part of this rule explains how to write a limerick. A limerick is a special, five-line poem in which certain lines rhyme with each other. Make sure that the correct lines rhyme! If you make any variations on this rhyming scheme, you will end up with something other than a limerick. Don't be disqualified simply because you didn't read the rules closely enough. Although a limerick is the most common type of poem you will encounter, you may be asked to write others. The rules will almost always explain the rhyming schemes of these poems.

RULE 3. *All entries must be postmarked February 29, 2004. You may enter as often as you like, but each entry must be mailed separately. Mail each entry to the address on the official entry blank.*

These rules indicate that the entries must be postmarked by a certain date, rather than received on that date. This simply means that you must get the entry into the mailbox by that date. Although the collection times for some mailboxes are as late as 6:30 PM, it would probably be best to drop it into the mailbox before noon. But I strongly advise against waiting until the very last day, just in case there is some kind of delay at the post office. These rules also indicate that all entries must be mailed separately. As with sweepstakes, you must not put all of your entries into a single envelope or package! If the contest does not stipulate which size envelope to use, then I recommend the #10 envelope (the long business envelope).
If you wish to enter more then once, then don't simply send in the same limerick several times. This is a game of skill, not of luck. Your chances of winning will only

increase if you send in more than one
limerick! I have heard of many people who,
not really understanding the difference
between a sweepstake and contest, simply
sent in the same entry over and over. If the
judges don't like it once, then they certainly
won't like it many times! There are an
infinite number of ways to complete the
three lines, so exercise your creativity and
complete it as many ways as possible.

This rule instructs you to mail your entry to
the address on the entry blank. If there is
more than one address, then don't worry.
You may remember that I explained the
reason for this in the RULES AND REGU-
LATIONS chapter for sweepstakes. You
should probably send at least one entry to
each address.

RULE 4. *Send the wrapper from a Yummy-
Yum candy with each entry.*

Remember that skill contests can require
you to include some kind of proof of purchase. There is no way around this, so don't
"accidentally" leave it out, or you will be

disqualified. Sometimes the rules specify a certain portion of the wrapper, such as the words "Yummy-Yum," so be careful to enclose the correct portion.

RULE 5. *All entries will be judged on the following criteria: Creativity-40%; Sincerity-30%; and Aptness-30%. The decisions of the judges are final.*

Contests usually specify the exact basis of their judgments. The criteria indicated above (all of which you now understand) are a good approximation of the ones you will probably encounter. If you remember to follow the simple SOS rule, and try to incorporate some of the techniques mentioned in the previous chapter, then you should have no trouble fulfilling the criteria. The final sentence of this rule, that all decisions are final, means that you should never bother appealing a decision. If you have lost a contest, then simply chalk it up to experience and enter a new one. Don't waste your time becoming embittered that you didn't win with an entry you thought was great. Remember, the judging process is very subjective.

RULE 6. *All entries become the property of the Yummy-Yum Candy Corporation. The contest is open to residents of the contiguous U.S.A. Void where prohibited. You must be at least 18 to enter. No employees of the Yummy-Yum Candy Corporation, the judging organization, or the families of such employees, are eligible. Limit one prize per family. No substitutions of prizes permitted. All prizes will be awarded. Duplicate prizes will be awarded in the case of a tie. Taxes are the responsibility of the prize winner. Entry constitutes permission to Yummy-Yum Candy Corporation for use of winners' names and photographs without further compensation.*

The first sentence of this rule means that the Yummy-Yum candy corporation will own your entry after you send it to them. Thus, if they decide to use your entry as the focus of their new ad campaign, then you are not entitled to any compensation; the most that you will get is a prize. The rest of this rule is comprised of the standard disclaimers: who may or may not enter, who must pay the taxes, how many prizes you can win, where it is legal and where it isn't, etc. As with sweepstakes, don't try to get away with cheating any part of this rule. If you are under the age requirement, then don't enter. If you live in a state where the contest is void, then don't enter. Don't try to cheat the contest sponsor, because you will be caught, and you won't receive a prize. As with most promotions, this contest prohibits you from substituting prizes. Note that this contest also stipulates that the sponsor can use your name and likeness as often as it wishes; this means that you may have to sit down for photographers if you win, and you may even see your face on the walls of the supermarket for many months.

RULE 7. *For a list of winners, send a separate self-addressed stamped envelope to the address on the official entry blank.*

As with sweepstakes, you can request a list of the winners. But remember that you will not receive a copy of their entries. It may take several months for you to receive this list. Never enclose the self-addressed stamped envelope for this list with your own entry blank, as this will result in your disqualification. Note that the rule specifically states to send it separately. This is true for all promotions, whether the rules indicate it or not.

Now that you understand the basic rules for a contest, I would like to discuss some suggestions that apply specifically to recipe contests. These suggestions will probably not appear in the rules themselves, but they are so important that you should essentially consider them rules.

SUGGESTION 1. *Give clear instructions.*

Don't try to be creative in the way you present your recipe. Just present it! The judges want a clear list of steps to follow in order to make your dish, not a prose paragraph detailing the history of cooking. Imagine if you were trying to assemble a piece of furniture and the instructions were difficult to read; you'd go crazy! That's pretty much how the judges feel when they don't receive a step-by-step list. If your recipe is not easy to follow, then you might as well consider yourself disqualified.

There is a standard format in which you should present your recipe. You should write the name of the recipe on the top line of the page, centered. Then skip three lines. Then list the ingredients in the order they should be used, *not* in order of relative importance. Then skip a few more lines and explain how to prepare the dish in straightforward, step-by-step sentences.

After completing the recipe, you should give it to one of your friends and see if they can make the dish. If they come back with any questions, or if they come back with something that looks nothing like your dish, then you should definitely rewrite the recipe.

SUGGESTION 2. *Give exact measurements.*

Personally, I'm the kind of cook who throws anything in a pot without stopping to think about precise measurements. For this reason I don't think I'll ever win a recipe contest, despite the fact that I *am* a pretty good cook. If you plan to be a recipe contest winner, then you must get into the habit of measuring exactly. Remember, the judges need to be able to reproduce your meal after reading the recipe, and if they are unsure of the proper quantities, then they will throw your entry in the garbage.

Remember to be as specific as possible in your measurements. If your recipe calls for one tablespoon of sugar, but your interpretation of a tablespoon is a huge scoop, then convert it into level tablespoons; your tablespoon, for example, may be two or three normal tablespoons. Never use personalized amounts, such as pinches or scoops, as they are different for everyone. If you use a pinch of salt, then measure it out in a spoon to see exactly how much it is.

Some other things for which you must give precise measurements are the size of your pots and the temperature at which your recipe should be cooked. If your recipe calls for an ambiguous quantity, such as two large onions, then you should cut up the onions and put them in a measuring cup. That way you can avoid any uncertain terms, such as "large"; instead of telling the judges to dice two large onions, for example, you should tell them to use two cups of diced onions. It is very easy to become over concerned with precision, as I am sure you will discover. But again, if you give the recipe to a friend, and the friend can make it, then you are probably being accurate enough.

SUGGESTION 3. *Neatness counts.*

I have already mentioned that recipe contests require a certain format, so follow it! Most contests ask you to type your recipe on a plain sheet of paper, 8 1/2 x 11". But, as with all promotions, you should read the rules carefully. Perhaps the contest you are entering wants the recipe on index cards, or perhaps it wants entries to be hand written. But whatever the format, whatever the style, make it neat! If you have a rickety old typewriter that can't print any vowels, then ask to borrow your friend's new word processor. If you have ugly hand printing, then ask your sister to print it out for you.

SUGGESTION 4. *Highlight the contest sponsor's product.*

When listing the ingredients, always type (or print) the name of the sponsor's product in capital letters. Furthermore, if you use more than the minimum amount of the product than the recipe calls for, then it is a good idea to highlight the amount as well. This is a somewhat sneaky way to catch the judges' attention, but it usually works.

You should also do a little bit of research to see what other products the company makes. For example, if the Yummy-Yum Candy Corporation is sponsoring a recipe contest in which you must use a pint of their chocolate ice cream, then look for other products made by Yummy-Yum that you can use (such as chopped nuts, chocolate syrup, etc.). Always highlight these ingredients as well as the required ingredient. Moreover, if you do some research to determine whether or not the sponsoring company is affiliated with any other companies, then you may discover more products to highlight. If, for example, you have a wonderful new recipe for a banana split, you may discover that Yummy-Yum owns the Daylight Fruit Company. You should then list in your ingredients not simply two cups of chopped bananas, but two cups of chopped DAYLIGHT FRUIT bananas.

This is another reason why using pre-packaged ingredients can be so helpful. You are likely to stumble upon many ingredients, such as soup stocks, which are also manufactured by the sponsoring company.

SUGGESTION 5. *Be careful when naming a recipe.*

You have to be very careful when giving your recipe a name. Some judges prefer recipes that have straightforward names, such as "The Yummy-Yum Banana Split," whereas others prefer something more creative, such as "Banana Ecstasy." In order to figure out which type of name is more appropriate for the contest you are entering, you should do some research. Have the winners of this contest usually had straightforward names, or have they challenged the judges to guess precisely what the dish is? Such research is the only way to be certain which kind of name to use.

Even when you are creative with names, however, you should always at least *suggest* what kind of a dish you are entering. In the previous paragraph, for example, I named a banana split recipe "Banana Ecstasy." In this case, the judges have some inkling as to the ingredients of the dish.

CHAPTER 10:
WHERE TO FIND CONTESTS

Now that you know several ways to improve your chances of winning contests, you are probably wondering how to enter them. As with sweepstakes, the three major avenues through which you can find out about contests are magazines, your local stores, and clubs.

If you are interested in recipe contests, then the magazines in which you can find the appropriate entry blanks are (naturally) such cooking and homemaking magazines as *Family Circle.* As recipe contests require so much research, it is imperative that you subscribe to one of these magazines, or at least be prepared to make frequent trips to the library. If possible, I would suggest subscribing to two or three magazines, as you will be able to examine a large variety of contests and winning recipes, allowing you to get a good sense of the kinds of dishes that are popular. I realize that this can become somewhat expensive, but it is well worth the cost; remember, contesting is a hobby that requires some investment.

Many of the word contests are advertised in

the same magazines as the recipe contests. This is because many companies that sponsor word contests are food companies. Therefore, if you wish to participate in both types of contests, your financial investment will not necessarily increase.

A good way to lower the cost of such subscriptions is by sharing them with a friend or relative. Perhaps you are interested in word contests, while your brother has a passion for recipe contests. Contesting (and sweepstaking, for that matter) is a hobby that can be shared with your entire family; this will not only reduce the costs of becoming a serious promotions entrant, but it can also be a way to share your time with your loved ones.

As with sweepstakes, most contests are also advertised at your local store. As far as cooking contests go, you will most likely find entry blanks in the larger national grocery stores; this is convenient, as these are the stores where you should shop for your ingredients. The entry blanks will usually be located near the products that are sponsoring the contest, or at the check-out stand, or in the store manager's office. Remember, companies view promotions as a great marketing device, so it should never be very difficult to find the appropriate entry blanks. And if you see a contest that you know you want to enter, don't forget to see if you are required to send in some kind of proof of purchase; if you don't already own the product, you might as well save yourself an extra trip by picking one up right then and there. If you enjoy entering both sweepstakes and contests, then you will probably find yourself being much more selective with the latter, as it can become very expensive to buy products indiscriminately.

And finally, the last place in which you can find out about contests is your local contest club. These clubs are generally even more popular than sweepstakes clubs, as members can actually share skills and practice with each other. In fact, the oldest promotion club in the country is a contest club.

Again, clubs do take the most time and

effort on your part, but they are certainly the most rewarding. And if you actually enjoy contesting, then there should be no reason for not spending lots of time at it. If there is not already such a club in your town, then you should definitely consider forming one. That way, you can make valuable contacts with whom you can share tips, and hopefully you can make some friends as well.

If you do decide to form a contest club, then remember that the most important activities you can organize are practice sessions. Each week, when you have club meetings, ask everyone to bring in a practice limerick for the other members to complete. You could establish specific criteria by which the limerick (or any other type of word contest, such as explaining why you use a certain product in twenty five words or less) will be judged. After everyone has completed the practice contest, you can decide on a winner and discuss why you felt that entry was the best.

Moreover, if you hold club meetings in

someone's house, then you can also practice recipe contests in the kitchen. Each week you can decide upon a specific ingredient around which to center the recipe, and then everyone can try to concoct the best dish off the top of their heads. By practicing in this fashion, you can assure yourself of the ability to create quick and easy dishes which anyone can prepare.

If your contest club really starts to blossom, then you could even consider inviting guest speakers, such as previous winners or spokespeople from companies that regularly sponsor contests. By doing this, you can learn valuable winning strategies and techniques. As you can see, a contest club can easily grow very large and offer many activities to improve your skills; your club could become a very rewarding organization for all of its members.

There are three national recipe contests that you should definitely be aware of. The first is the Pillsbury Bake-Off Contest. This is the single most famous cooking contest in the country, and you have probably already heard of it, but I would like to discuss it briefly at this point. The top prize is a cash award in the tens of thousands of dollars, and there are several other generous runner-up cash awards as well. There are four categories in which you can enter (you *can* enter in as many as you like): refrigerated dinner roll, refrigerated biscuit, flour, and package mix. This is the contest that you *must* enter each year, as the potential awards are so high.

The second is the National Pineapple Cooking Contest, in which semi-finalists are flown to Hawaii in order to prepare their recipes for the judges! Again, the prizes are astronomically generous. And the third is the National Chicken Cooking Contest, in which semi-finalists are chosen from each state to compete in a final cook-off against each other. All three of these contests are gala events that you wouldn't want to miss. Be on the lookout for information and entry blanks in all the places that have been discussed in this chapter!

There are other well respected national

contests that you will read about when doing your research in magazines and grocery stores, but you should also remember that local organizations, religious groups, and schools often hold recipe contests. While you obviously won't win huge cash awards from these smaller promotions, you might win some nice prizes, and you can definitely practice your skills.

OTHER INFORMATION YOU SHOULD KNOW ABOUT PROMOTIONS

CHAPTER 11:
YOU'RE A WINNER!

So you've spent all of your free time gathering the necessary supplies, reading the rules thoroughly, entering any sweepstake or contest you could find, browsing through magazines, searching the aisles of supermarkets, practicing your rhyming skills, concocting magnificent new recipes, joining clubs, and networking with people who share your passion for promotions . . . And guess what?

You won!

That's right, you won. All of your efforts actually paid off, and you are the proud possessor of a cash prize, or a new car, or a boat, or even a home in the woods. You couldn't be happier. All of your friends come over to congratulate you and pat you on the back. You deserve to be proud of yourself, because you have truly accomplished something special, something that most people only dream of.

So what's next? Well the first thing that you should expect is to be visited by a private detective agency, but there is no need for you to worry. If you look back to the chapters of this book that dealt with the rules of sweepstakes and competitions, then you will remember that they always include a few disclaimers, such as void where prohibited. The reason that the sponsoring company hires a private detective is so that they can be absolutely positive that you have complied with all of the rules. If you have done so, then you have nothing to worry about. The detectives cannot declare that you do not deserve the prize, or that you deserve a lesser prize, as long as you have not broken the rules. It would be illegal for them to do so, even if they don't like you, so don't panic.

This is why it is so important for you never to break the rules; you will be caught. If you are nineteen years old, and the contest states you must be over twenty one, then you will be disqualified, and you will *not* receive your prize. If your estranged fourth cousin, twice removed, works for the Yummy-Yum Candy Corporation, then don't bother entering any of their contests or sweepstakes, because you will be disqualified. It is the detective agency's responsibility to find these things out, and they are very thorough in their investigations.

Many people ask why sponsoring companies don't allow their employees, or relatives of their employees, to enter their promotions. The answer to this is simple. Remember how dubious you were of sweepstakes and contests before reading this book? Well imagine how dubious people would be if even just one of the company's employees won a major prize; no one would believe that the promotions were on the level, and the sponsoring company's credibility would be destroyed. Rather than allow for the possibility of this happening, the companies simply forbid their employees from entering.

The detective who visits you will probably ask you to sign an affidavit swearing that you followed all of the rules. Never refuse to sign this affidavit, or you could be disqualified. Never refuse to see the detective, and never answer any of his questions falsely. You wouldn't want to be disqualified and lose your prize simply because you panicked. If you have followed all the rules, then you have nothing to worry about! The affidavit that you will be given is extremely straightforward; it essentially says that you promise that you followed all the rules. I have never heard of anyone hiring a lawyer to read the affidavit, and I certainly don't think you will need one. But, if you do win, it probably cannot hurt to give your lawyer a call and ask his advice *before* meeting with the detective.

There is only one bad thing about winning: taxes. I have only heard of one or two promotions in my entire life in which the taxes were paid for the winner by the sponsoring company, so be prepared to cough up some dough. This is why you should be at least somewhat selective in which promotions you enter. In fact, the taxes on a large prize can sometimes be as high as seventy percent.

"Seventy percent!" did you cry in anguish? Well the only way to make yourself feel better about this is to remember that you're not losing money; at the very least, you're *winning* thirty percent of a prize. You should never try to weasel your way out of paying your fair share in taxes, as painful as it may seem to do so, because you could get into a lot of trouble. At the very least you could wind up paying a fine, in which case almost all of your prize money will be taken away from you, and you could even be sent to jail. Is it really worth going to jail in order to avoid paying a few hundred dollars in taxes? But it is understandable that you should want to pay as little as possible. I cannot advise you on how to accomplish that, however, as tax laws are so complicated. The best I can do is tell you to see a reputable tax lawyer or accountant.

If the prize that you win is cash, then you simply have to declare the *exact* amount in your income taxes. If the prize is merchandise, then things become slightly more complicated. You must declare the *fair market value* of the item. Fair market value does not mean wholesale value or retail value; it means the amount that a seller, not forced to sell, can demand, and a buyer, not forced to buy, will pay.

If you win a home that costs somewhere around fifty thousand dollars, you cannot "sell" it to your wife for five bucks, and then pay taxes on this amount. Five dollars is clearly not the fair market value of this home. Fair market value, once the home has been appraised, will no doubt be in the vicinity of fifty thousand dollars. This is the amount you must declare, whether you decide to sell it or not.

But what happens if you win some really ugly curtains that retail for $2000. If you try to sell them, and no one is willing to pay more than $300 for them, then the fair market value might turn out to be around $300. While discrepancies this large rarely occur, people have sometimes had trouble selling their prizes for their full value. This is especially true in the case of customized furniture which would have to be reupholstered to fit into anyone else's house, and in the case of "incomplete" prizes, such as a trip to Acapulco which doesn't include the airfare.

Sometimes it is absolutely impossible to find a buyer, and you are stuck with a prize that you really don't want. In this case, the fair market value you declare will be very low. But don't try to get away with declaring the ugly curtains at ten dollars, because the IRS might not agree with you. In a case such as this, it is best for you to consult your tax lawyer or an IRS agent. Such agents understand that fair market value can be difficult to ascertain, and they are usually very willing to help you determine a reasonable amount to declare. At the very least, they will probably point you in the direction of certain periodicals and catalogs in which you can find the prices of similar items. So your homework isn't over, even after you've won.

As with other forms of income, you can make certain deductions on your winnings. But you can never actually declare a loss. For example, if you can only sell your $2000 curtains for $300, you may *not* claim a loss of $1700. You have gained at least $300 from this promotion, and you must pay the taxes on that gain. But what kinds of deductions can you make?

You can deduct nearly everything that helped you become a winner. You can deduct the cost of postage stamps, paper, pencils, dictionaries, thesauruses, and the subscriptions to magazines. You may not, however, deduct the cost of the items you had to buy in order to enter contests, as these items are considered part of your personal expenses. This is yet another reason why you should choose your contests carefully; you don't want to be stuck with a hundred boxes of stale Yummy-Yum cereal when you can't even get a tax break on them.

And finally, you must remember that you can only make these deductions if you actually *win* a promotion. If you do not win, you are entitled to *no* deductions, even if you have spent hundreds of dollars gathering supplies and purchasing products. Remember, a deduction can only be made against a legitimate source of income, and if you don't win, then you receive no income from promotions.

If you do win, you are going to find yourself at the center of attention for some time. Not only will your friends and family be phoning all day and night to congratulate you, but you may actually be interviewed by television or newspaper reporters. The sponsoring company will almost definitely send representatives to congratulate you and take your photograph. You might even see a huge photo of yourself at the supermarket the next time you go shopping.

All of this can be quite daunting to unsuspecting winners. But if you keep your head, then you can actually enjoy your brief moments of fame. Unfortunately, too many people get nervous when they are barraged by friends, neighbors, and reporters, so they forget how much fun they could be having by receiving all this attention.

If you live in a small town, then it is quite likely that the whole town will know about your victory within a few days. The local newspaper will probably run a huge story about you. Chances are, you will receive many phone calls from churches, schools, elderly centers, and other local groups asking for donations, particularly if you won a large cash award. I realize that this may seem like an invasion of your privacy, but I would urge you to consider donating at least a small amount to any of these groups. The only reason they are calling is because they are legitimately short of funding, so why not share some of your good fortune with them? At the very least, you will get a warm and rewarding feeling in your heart. And, if you are careful about selecting which groups you wish to help out, you might be able to ensure that your donations are tax deductible.

If you live in a large city, then it is unlikely that you will be the subject of any major newspaper articles, unless you win a really huge promotion. But you will still find that word of your victory somehow gets out. You may even find your mailbox stuffed with letters from people all over the city, asking you to help them out of their own hard financial times. I cannot give you any sound advice on how to deal with these letters, except to say that there are many people who attempt to take advantage of the fortunate. You must make your own decisions about them. In the past, some winners have found it useful to change their phone number to an unlisted number, and some have also gotten P.O. boxes in order to filter out unwanted letters.

If you win one of the large contests, then you could very well be interviewed by some of the same magazines that you subscribed to in order to win. And with the recent rise in the popularity of daytime talk shows, there is even a chance you could be on TV. If you win one of the national recipe contests, then your recipe will certainly be published in magazines, and it may even appear on the labels of cans and other products. Your grandmother's prized recipe for spaghetti sauce could end up a household favorite across the country!

Ironically, many people actually become depressed upon winning a large prize. They feel guilty for their sudden good fortune. While I am no psychologist, let me assure you that such feelings are completely normal; don't let them depress you!

Remind yourself that you worked hard to win this prize, that it wasn't simply a random accident, and that you deserved it. After winning, some people feel empty inside. This is akin to postpartum depression, or the sadness mothers sometimes feel after giving birth. If you spend months, or even years, of your life working toward a goal, you suddenly feel like you have nothing left to do once that goal is achieved. Again, this is completely normal, so don't let it worry you. The best cure for such depression is to resume your hobby immediately. Just because you've won one promotion, why should that stop you from entering another? Of course, the other cure is to simply have fun and enjoy your good fortune!

Some big winners have literally found themselves leading normal lives one day, and having the lifestyles of Hollywood movie stars the next. Fame and fortune has a way of sweeping the unsuspecting away, changing their lives in ways that make them sad, and somehow getting in the way of their happiness. Don't let this happen to you! If you keep your head on your shoulders, then a cash award or other prize could help you live the life of your dreams. If you feel uncomfortable as a minor celebrity, then don't become a minor celebrity. Do only the bare minimum number of interviews and photo sessions. If you enjoy the sudden attention, then bask in it. The point is, don't let your victory control you. As long as you control it, then it should never result in anything but happiness.

CONCLUSION

By now, I am sure you have realized that you must devote a fair amount of time and effort in order to be a serious sweepstakes or contest entrant. Hopefully, you now realize that being a winner doesn't simply hinge upon whether or not you are lucky. A winner plays the game skillfully, entering often and playing efficiently. That is why the same people seem to win contests and sweepstakes over and over again.

Although there is no way that I can guarantee you will become a winner, if you follow the suggestions I have outlined in this book, then your chances of winning should improve dramatically. It is very possible that you could become the next big winner, living the life of your dreams.

But I want to remind you of something I mentioned at the beginning of this book. As long as you are enjoying the time you spend entering promotions, then you are always winning. It might take a tremendous amount of effort to start a contest club in your town, but isn't it worth it? The new friends you make and the new skills you learn are rewards that certainly make the effort worthwhile. I cannot think of a single hobby that does not demand a great deal of effort. So, in your quest to become a "winner," don't forget to enjoy the thrill of playing. And if you are a contest lover, then don't forget to enjoy improving your writing, cooking, or other skills.

If you only remember two things from this book, then they should be: (1) follow the rules exactly; and (2) enter as often as possible.

You should be proud of yourself. You are now aware of a legitimate form of income that most people simply don't understand. So the next time your friend drops a comment like, "No one ever wins those things," or "They only give prizes to people who buy something," you can set them straight. You might even want to loan them this book.

Many people are afraid to change their lives. Many people are truly scared of success, as if the newfound responsibilities outweigh the newfound rewards. Don't fall into this trap! Grab any opportunity for success that comes your way. This is true not only in the case of promotions, but for all other aspects of life as well.

Most books such as this end with the words, "Good luck!" But I won't use these words, because by now we both understand that luck is one of the least important factors in winning sweepstakes and contests. Instead, I'd like to sign off with: "Good work. You're one step closer to winning already!"